Dead Man's Float

Also by Jim Harrison

Jim Harrison

DEAD
MAN'S
FLOAT

Copper Canyon Press
Port Townsend, Washington

Cover art: Russell Chatham, *Hayfields on the Cottonwood Bench,* 2004. Oil, 36" × 48".

Copper Canyon Press is in residence at Fort Worden State Park in Port Townsend, Washington, under the auspices of Centrum. Centrum is a gathering place for artists and creative thinkers from around the world, students of all ages and backgrounds, and audiences seeking extraordinary cultural enrichment.

LIBRARY OF CONGRESS CATALOGING-IN-PUBLICATION DATA

Harrison, Jim, 1937–
[Poems. Selections]
Dead man's float / Jim Harrison.
pages ; cm
ISBN 978-1-55659-445-8 (hardcover : acid-free paper)
I. Title.
PS3558.A67A6 2015
811'.54 – dc23
2015017095

3 5 7 9 8 6 4 2

FIRST EDITION

COPPER CANYON PRESS
Post Office Box 271
Port Townsend, Washington 98368

www.coppercanyonpress.org

In memory of Valerie de la Valdene

ACKNOWLEDGMENTS

Poems from *Dead Man's Float* originally appeared in the following publications:
The Café Review, Elk River Books Reader, Lost Roads, Narrative, Nothing to Declare
(White Pine Press), *Reflections* (Yale Divinity School), *Talking River,* and *Tantré Farm
Digest.* I like that *Tantré Farm Digest* was given out free at the Farmers Market in
Ann Arbor. Thanks, also, to Garrison Keillor and his radio program *The Writer's
Almanac* – a friendly voice in the wilderness if ever there was one.

The epigraph for "Moon Suite" is the first stanza of Federico García Lorca's poem
"Romance de la luna, luna," and is translated by Helen Gunn.

Contents

Dead Man's Float

Where Is Jim Harrison?

He fell off the cliff of a seven-inch *zafu*.
He couldn't get up because of his surgery.
He believes in the Resurrection mostly
because he was never taught how not to.

Hospital

I was chest-high in the wheat field with wind blowing in shimmering circles. A girl on horseback came by on a trail and the horse smelled sweet with the wheat. How blessed horses smell in this bitter world.

I could see the hospital in the distance and imagined the surgeons in the basement sharpening their knives. Tomorrow they will cut me from neck bone to tailbone to correct mysterious imperfections that keep me from walking. I want to walk like other kids in the fields with my noble dog.

After surgery I didn't get well and they sent me to Mayo in Minnesota, an immense Pentagon of health machinery. In an ambulance-plane I ate a bad sandwich in keeping with the tradition of bad food that would last until my secretary brought takeout from a nearby restaurant.

Each night I sang along with a bedsore cantata from the endless halls, the thousand electronic gizmos beeping, and also people entering my room for "tests." I was endlessly sacrificed at the medical gizmo altar. There was no red wine and no cigarettes – only the sick who tore at the heart.

A beautiful girl Payton couldn't walk. I'd shudder whenever I passed her room.

On very long sleepless nights I'd gaze at the well-lit statue of Saint Francis across the courtyard. I'm not Catholic but he bore me up with birds on his shoulders. One night the planet Venus dropped unwelcome on his neck. Francis with Venus is not right. I don't think he knew a woman. I saw the same thing in Narbonne, France, one night with a million blackbirds flocking above the canal for the trip south across the Mediterranean. Venus was blurred on the peak of the cathedral.

My spine aches from top to bottom. Also my shingles burn, a special punishment. Francis heard my crying over Payton. He doesn't care about her beauty I suppose. There were no beauty contests among his birds.

I heard Mozart's last trio late last night, a spine-tickler, like the night I heard Thelonious Monk in Grand Central. There are so many emotions on earth, especially trapped here where moment by moment I surge with emotions. I'm told this place is admired throughout the world, though my brain waves tell me different. The nurses are kind and friendly while the doctors tend toward smug and arrogant. Hundreds of doctors looking for something wrong are suspicious.

The old bugaboo of depression slid in. I wanted to sleep on the floor but was frozen in an electric bed. I began to have delusions and at one point I was in Paris at my favorite food store buying cheeses with my grandson. Another night I was wailing and the attendant shook me awake. "I'm dying," I said. "No you're not, you're just wailing." I ate an apple and went back to staring at Saint Francis and his birds. Without birds I'm dead. They are my drug that lifts me up to flight. Thousands of kinds of birds I've studied, even in the rain when they seem more blessed on the branches.

What *is* wailing? A death-drawn crooning. It hurts to hear noises from the pediatric ward – the innocent crying out. I am thoroughly guilty in a long life.

I wanted to be a cello. I hear cellos when I'm trout fishing. The green banks with wild roses capture the cellos and thousands of birds, many sweet-sounding warblers and colorful western tanagers. Will I fish again with this badly ruptured spine? The scar looks like the bite of an ancient creature.

There is a place in us to weep for others. I found it at night with daytime eyes, whirling the memories so fresh you could smell the pain within is dark and raw. This great sprawl of sick people craving the outside, to walk in a forest beside a lake, the air full of birds in the greenery. Saint Francis dozing against a tree, a yellow warbler perched on his shoulder. There is no way out of this prison we have built so clumsily, hellish in its ugliness. Most of us want to stay. I can't die when I want to go back to Narbonne and my secret room where I write so much. They cut me open in a long strip and luckily sewed me back up. In hospitals we are mostly artful sewage systems.

I need my secret place in the Upper Peninsula near Lake Superior, my dark thicket covered by winter. It is night in there but I can watch passing animals, a deer, bear, even possums, which I love for their humility. The thicket is flooded with birds, a few inches from my good eye. Francis would love this thicket. Maybe I'll take him there someday. And best of all a stump in a gully that I can crawl into and sit up. My place of grace on earth, my only church. The gods live there.

How to get out of this hospital? I planned three departures but a doctor won't sign my release. I am desperate for home and my lovely wife. They want to keep me here though departure is supposedly voluntary. Finally a friend in California sent a jet and saved me. We loaded up my daughter, my secretary, and her daughter and were soaring back to Montana.

A green glade of soft marsh grass near a pool in a creek. There are a dozen white birches and I curl in the grass. The last day I saw a drop of blood on a tile. Be careful, our blood falls easily.

Birds

The birds are flying around frantically
in the thunderstorm that just began, the
first in weeks and weeks. They are enjoying
themselves. I think I'll join them.

Solstice Litany

1

The Saturday morning meadowlark
came in from high up
with her song gliding into tall grass
still singing. How I'd like
to glide around singing in the summer
then to go south to where I already was
and find fields full of meadowlarks
in winter. But when walking my dog
I want four legs to keep up with her
as she thunders down the hill at top speed
then belly flops into the deep pond.
Lark or dog I crave the impossible.
I'm just human. All too human.

2

I was nineteen and mentally
infirm when I saw the prophet Isaiah.
The hem of his robe was as wide
as the horizon and his trunk and face
were thousands of feet up in the air.
Maybe he appeared because I had read him
so much and opened too many ancient doors.
I was cooking my life in a cracked clay
pot that was leaking. I had found
secrets I didn't deserve to know.
When the battle for the mind is finally
over it's late June, green and raining.

3

A violent windstorm the night before
the solstice. The house creaked and yawned.
I thought the morning might bring a bald earth,
bald as a man's bald head but not shiny.
But dawn was fine with a few downed trees,
the yellow rosebush splendidly intact.
The grass was all there dotted with Black
Angus cattle. The grass is indestructible
except to fire but now it's too green to burn.
What did the cattle do in this storm?
They stood with their butts toward the wind,
erect Buddhists waiting for nothing in particular.
I was in bed cringing at gusts,
imagining the contents of earth all blowing
north and piled up where the wind stopped,
the pile sky-high. No one can climb it.
A gopher comes out of a hole as if nothing happened.

4

The sun should be a couple of million miles
closer today. It wouldn't hurt anything
and anyway this cold rainy June is hard
on me and the nesting birds. My own nest
is stupidly uncomfortable, the chair
of many years. The old windows don't keep
the weather out, the wet wind whipping
my hair. A very old robin drops dead
on the lawn, a first for me. Millions
of birds die but we never see it – they like
privacy in this holy, fatal moment or so
I think. We can't tell each other when we die.

Others must carry the message to and fro.
"He's gone," they'll say. While writing an average poem
destined to disappear among the millions of poems
written now by mortally average poets.

5

Solstice at the cabin deep in the forest.
The full moon shines in the river, there are pale
green northern lights. A huge thunderstorm
comes slowly from the west. Lightning strikes
a nearby tamarack bursting into flame.
I go into the cabin feeling unworthy.
At dawn the tree is still smoldering
in this place the gods touched earth.

Another Country

I love these raw moist dawns with
a thousand birds you hear but can't
quite see in the mist.
My old alien body is a foreigner
struggling to get into another country.
The loon call makes me shiver.
Back at the cabin I see a book
and am not quite sure what that is.

Zona

My work piles up,
I falter with disease.
Time rushes toward me –
it has no brakes. Still,
the radishes are good this year.
Run them through butter,
add a little salt.

Seven in the Woods

Am I as old as I am?
Maybe not. Time is a mystery
that can tip us upside down.
Yesterday I was seven in the woods,
a bandage covering my blind eye,
in a bedroll Mother made me
so I could sleep out in the woods
far from people. A garter snake glided by
without noticing me. A chickadee
landed on my bare toe, so light
she wasn't believable. The night
had been long and the treetops
thick with a trillion stars. Who
was I, half-blind on the forest floor
who was I at age seven? Sixty-eight
years later I can still inhabit that boy's
body without thinking of the time between.
It is the burden of life to be many ages
without seeing the end of time.

Easter Again

Christ rose so long ago but the air
he rose through hasn't forgotten
the slight red contrail from the wounds.
I think he was headed
to that galaxy with six trillion stars
to cool off from the Crucifixion.
I have often heard the spikes
being driven through hands
and feet – in my mind, that is.
The sky was truly dark blue
that day and earth a tiny
green-and-blue ball.

The Present

I'm sitting on the lip of this black hole, a well
that descends to the center of the earth.
With a big telescope aimed straight down
I see a red dot of fire and hear the beast howling.
My back is suppurating with disease,
the heart lurches left and right,
the brain sings its ditties.
Everywhere blank white movies wait to be seen.
The skylark flew within inches of the rocks
before it stopped and rose again.
The cost of flight is landing.

Soul

My spirit is starving.
How can it be fed?
Not by pain in the predictable future
nor the pain in the past
but understanding the invisible flower
within the flower that tells it what is,
the soul of the tree that does the same.
I don't seem to have a *true character*
to discover, a man slumped on his desk
dozing at midmorning. I'm an old poet.
That's it. Period. A three-legged goat
in mountain country. It's easier in the woods
where you have trees to lean on. There at times
I smelled bears right behind the cabin
coming to eat sunflower seeds put out for birds.
This dawn it's primroses, penstemon,
the trellis of white roses. On Easter
Jesus is Jesus. When did God enter him or us?

Thunder

Thunder before dawn,
thunder through dawn,
thunder beings they were called.
It had to be a person or animal up there.
Outside, walking to my work shed
the clouds were low, almost black, and turbulent.
You could nearly jump up and touch them.
I love thunder. I could listen to it all day long.
Like birdsong it's the music of the gods.
How in childhood I adored these cloud voices
that could lift me up above my troubles,
far above the birds. I'd look down
at their flying backs, always in circles
because earth is round. What a gift
to have my work shed shudder with thunder.

Reverse Prayer

I pray for Mandelstam hiding covered
with snow in a ditch. The Stalinists want to kill
him and finally succeed. I want him to escape
to Nebraska, please God. I pray for Lorca
that the assassin's guns won't work and he'll
escape like a heron flying west to the Mediterranean
then across the ocean to Michigan where he might
dislike the snow but at least he's alive.
He loved Cuba and Brazil for their music which
we don't have much of here. Please God, save him.
I even pray for Keats that he won't die
so young but get another thirty years or so
to write poems in Rome. He likes
sitting with my girlfriend on the Spanish
Steps. Can I trust him? Probably not
but I want more of his poems so I'll overlook
his behavior. And of course Caravaggio
the king of painters must live longer,
God. Why create a great painter
then let him die early?

A Ballad of Love and Death about Elsa

The ambulance driver told me in a bar
about the car accident – Elsa's head torn off
and her eyes stayed open.
I went to the site with a bouquet of flowers.
The road's shoulder was short green grass and along
the fence there were primroses and California
poppies. In the field a brown-and-white cow
watched me wander around. I wondered
how long Elsa could see, and what.
I found a patch of blood-crisp grass
where her head must have rested
surrounded by shards of windshield.
She was a fine gardener with a sweet,
warm voice.

Molly the Brave

Molly was the bravest.
In April she would swing out
over the river on a rope
tied to an elm branch. There was still
ice along the bank and one day
her body was found down by the weir
with a bruised head, which meant she hit ice.
One summer evening she hugged me in her wet
black bathing suit after I brought her a milk shake.
My blood became hot and moved in all directions.
When we caught frogs to eat their legs
she said, "We are animals." And on the hill
by the river we illegally picked trillium.
All the boys wanted to marry her.
We kept putting the wildflowers she loved
on her grave. More than sixty years
later I see clearly that no one gets over anything
least of all Molly by the river,
swinging up through the air –

a bird.

Report from Valencia

The girl ran across the cemetery
with the wind at her back looking
for the empty grave she commissioned. She ran
the same speed as the wind so that the air
around her was still. She threw
herself weeping into the empty hole
screaming to be covered with soil.
Four boys who had been smoking dope
threw handfuls of dirt on her
and one small rock hit her on the head
and subdued her. She curled up
on the damp earth. This happened on the
outskirts of Valencia in Spain. Her lover
had left her. He wanted to go to America
and become rich and have a new car.
Compared to old Spain America is a new car.
She wanted to stay in Valencia and have
a baby. Eventually, the gravedigger came
along and said he couldn't bury her
without a government-stamped death certificate.
He helped her out of the grave with his rope ladder,
peeking up her legs.

Wood and War

Way back in the forest a dozen miles south of my log cabin there's a cabin on a high finger into a swamp with no path. Long ago a trapper lived there with a wife and three sons who went to World War II. Only one came home and lived the rest of his life in seclusion. The father was an ex-professor who died by freezing after breaking both hips running his snowmobile into a tree. The mother, batty and mute, lived in Duluth with her sister. Little Walter, the last son, was all that was left and starved himself to death in twenty years. Hunters and wanderers knew enough to stop by and help him cut and haul in wood. Winter got as low as 40 below. All the locals knew he was dying slow. Women sent out casseroles but the casseroles ended up with the bears. Walter had a bag of beans and a bag of rice. "O my brothers lost in war," he'd think, his heart broken in half by their absence. In February he was found naked, frozen, draped over his dwindled woodpile.

He looked like wood.

Sticking to It

The old Finn hadn't washed his cup
in fifty years. "It ain't dirty,"
he said, "there just been coffee in it."
His wife and baby both died in childbirth
fifty-seven years ago. Inside his cabin
there's a dust woman near
an unused cradle he made by hand.

Warmth

The lettuce pushed up through the cold, cold ground.
There is this relentless struggle for warmth on earth.
Mandelstam lay in the snowy ditch
in an outsized ratty black overcoat
hearing a troika go past with harness bells,
the thud of horse hooves. His face
was cold so he pulled his head down
into darkness like a turtle.
A piece of bread would have helped.
Recently in Nebraska a pretty girl
got lost in a blizzard and froze to death.
They fail to revive so many of us
in these halls of ice. So many drunks
freeze to death in Russia it's a public
scandal. They're tripling the price
of vodka to keep the poor from dying drunk.
So many American Indians freeze
walking home from bars on the reservation edge.
A friend died leaning and dozing against
his mailbox, so near home.

Cow

A cow is screaming across the arroyo.
It's a blasting Warsaw Ghetto scream.
It speaks of the end of time on earth.
I know her calf didn't die,
a little bull standing off to the side
staring at her with a "What's wrong with Mom?"
look. Next morning she's dead,
already smelling badly in the heat.
I think of the Bishop of Lyon in the ninth century
who said animals don't go to heaven because
they don't contribute to the church.
I see that the cow dogs are getting ready to eat her.
I see her spirit struggling to ascend to heaven.
That's no lie. I help her push off,
lifting her big head above a mass of bugs.

Seventy-Four

I can't be seventy-four.
It's plainly impossible.
Is this a near-death experience?
At dawn there were layers and layers
of birdsong from multiple willow thickets,
and an irritable kingfisher on the phone line
over the creek. They are always irritable
in my memory's storehouse of creeks, rivers,
lakes. "Get out of here! This is my place!"
they shriek. The Mexican green kingfisher
says the same thing. Such anger at dawn.
Meanwhile seventy-four years of birds
have passed. Most have died of course
so I shouldn't complain about the nearing
end of it all. I once saw a bird fall out
of a tree stone dead. I nudged it surprised
at its feather lightness that allowed it to fly.
I buried it in earth where they don't belong
any more than we do. Dead birds should be
monuments suspended forever in the air.

Old Man

An old man is a spindly junk pile.
He is so brittle he can fall
through himself top to bottom.
No mirror is needed to see the layers
of detritus, some years clogged with it.
The red bloody layer of auto deaths
of dad and sister. Deaths piled like cordwood
at the cabin, the body 190 pounds of ravaged
nerve ends from disease. The junk pile is without
sympathy for itself. A life is a life,
lived among birds and forests and fields.
It knew many dogs, a few bears and wolves.
Some women said they wanted to murder him
but what is there worth murdering?
The body, of course, the criminal body
doing this and that. Some will look
for miraculous gold nuggets in the junk
and find a piece of fool's gold in the empty
cans of menudo, a Mexican tripe stew.

Risen

We were so happy when the pretty girl
rose from the dead.
It was just past lilac time and the scent still hung
in the air like the death of the gods.
She didn't stay around for long. Once you've
been dead you're not happy to return.
She had been to the ends of the universe
and back and was a bit unearthly,
a bit too luminous to have a hamburger
or go running in the dark.

NYC

Hot, hungry, eighteen and reading
Lorca's *Poet in New York*.
Scholars say he lost his duende in NYC.
I don't think so. He got it back in Harlem,
then Havana. I walked three months
until my soles became paper and
I finally understood *Poet in New York*.
Homesick, I went home and worked on a farm.
Homesick, he went home and got murdered.

A Variation on Machado

I worry much about the suffering
of Machado. I was only one when he carried
his mother across the border from Spain to France
in a rainstorm. She died and so did he
a few days later in a rooming house along a dry canal.
To carry Mother he abandoned a satchel
holding his last few years of poetry.
I've traveled to Collioure several times
to search for Machado's lost satchel.
The French fed him but couldn't save him.
There's no true path to a death –
we discover the path by walking.
We turn a corner on no road
and there's a house on a green hill
with a thousand colorful birds sweeping in a circle.
Are the poems in the basement of the house on the hill?
We'll find out if we remember earth at all.

Vows

I feel my failure intensely
as if it were a vital organ
the gods grew from the side of my head.
You can't cover it with a hat and I no longer
can sleep on that side it's so tender.
I wasn't quite faithful enough
to carry this sort of weight up the mountain.
When I took my vows at nineteen
I had no idea that gods were so merciless.
Fear makes for good servants
and bravery is fraudulent. When I awoke
I wasn't awake enough.

Purple

It's criminal to claim you've earned
a Purple Heart if you didn't.
Politicians do this. I say, "Off with their heads."
Last spring in our bushy front yard
two mountain lions, mother and son
killed a deer – the leftovers of the meal were strikingly
red. I claim the Red Heart medal for inspecting
the carcass on this dangerous field of battle.
One took a mouthful then ripped
out the heart, stripping veins and arteries.
Lions with bloody faces, then ravens with bloody
beaks, about twenty yelling out victory
when the lions left. Once in Tanzania
I saw a big male lion with bloodred mane and face
after he had his whole head in the innards
of a zebra. He ignored us and the flies,
dozing with a full tummy in the midday heat.
I'm sharing the Red Heart medal with this lion.

Spirit

Rumi advised me to keep my spirit
up in the branches of a tree and not peek
out too far, so I keep mine in the very tall
willows along the irrigation ditch out back,
a safe place to remain unspoiled by the filthy
culture of greed and murder of the spirit.
People forget their spirits easily suffocate
so they must keep them far up in tree
branches where they can be summoned any moment.
It's better if you're outside as it's hard for spirits
to get into houses or buildings or airplanes.
In New York City I used to reach my spirit in front
of the gorilla cage in the children's zoo in Central Park.
It wouldn't come in the Carlyle Hotel, which
was too expensive for its taste. In Chicago
it won't come in the Drake though I can see it
out the window hovering over the surface
of Lake Michigan. The spirit above anything
else is attracted to humility. If I slept
in the streets it would be under the cardboard with me.

Wolves of Heaven

It had been very hot for three weeks
so I worked well into a cool night
when at three a.m. a big thunderstorm hit.
I went out in the yard naked and sat
at the picnic table for a rain bath
careful about the rattlesnake on the sidewalk.
The sky drowned the mosquitoes
feeding on me. The lightning was relentless
and lit up the valley so I could see
the ghosts who had me ill this past year.
Then I was part of a battle from two
hundred years ago when the Cheyenne
from the east attacked the Absaroka,
the Crow, in this valley. A group of the Cheyenne
were *massaum,* the wolves of heaven,
warriors who painted themselves solid yellow.
One on a black horse stopped at our gate
but decided not to kill me.
I want to be a yellow wolf of heaven.
They disappeared into the lightning.

Lost Medicine

I lost my medicine bag
from back when I believed
in magic. It's made from a doe's stomach
and holds a universe:
grizzly teeth and claw, stones from Tibet,
the moon, the garden, the beach
where the baby's ashes are buried.
Now I expect this bag to cure my illnesses –
I can't walk and the skin on my back
pulses and moans without a mouth.
The gods exiled me into this loneliness
of pain for their own good reasons.

Private Diamonds

Pain guides our lives very well.
Take the stone from your shoe
and by a miracle it replaces itself,
a private diamond. The peony buds
know exactly who they are and say so.

Lazuli Trance

I had to skin a 12 lb pork shank
which is a tough job if you're not a butcher.
Even when dead, animals want to keep their skin.
Antelope, deer, and bear are far easier than pigs.
So is a cow. I must have wanted to keep
the molar I had jerked the other day. It took
an hour to wrestle the sucker out by which time
I had entered the body of a lazuli bunting
back home twenty miles away. In bad times trances
help. The bird was marvelous as my bones had
never been so light though the new vision
was a little frightening but far from the dentist's office.
During my recent ninety days of shingles
I was in many creatures and many places.
You still inhabit the pain but are not miserably
trapped in its location. So my precious tooth
is gone forever, and I praise the lazuli bunting,
its miraculous colors of blue, a little white,
a chest patch of beige and orange, for taking
me to a far better place to suffer.

> (Author's advice: Choose small
> creatures, birds, salamanders, otter.
> Megafauna are dangerous
> and are far beyond the capabilities
> of almost anyone.)

Mountain Travel

The clouds are unmoving near Cambria
but the mountain I am on
drifts south with the wind,
a new way to travel, riding
a mountain as a horse made
of stone and earth. Only a few
miles but enough to flush a condor
from the ridge, the shadow passing
near my feet, the bird glancing at me
asking, "What are you doing here?"
I was a little frightened nestled
beneath a Santa Lucia fir, cushioning
my head on a giant cone,
wary of rattlesnakes among wildflowers
but had read of this experience in Buddhism
before Christ, hermits riding mountains.
Did people stop walking on water
or riding mountains after Christ?
What is a man to do if he can't ride mountains?
Tomorrow a walk upriver on the water.
Meanwhile, the earth flowed beneath my feet.
A round river floating in the sky.

God's Mouth

The girl thought that the sky was God's
wide-open mouth. After discussion, arguing,
I decided to agree. She was so sure
of herself, adamant in fact, as if stomping
a foot made anything true. I suppose
that at the back of the mouth is the brain
that created insects and galaxies, the girl
herself who is now singing a banal popular song
in a thin reedy voice. Then she told me
about a huge African catfish who keeps
her unruly children in her mouth. They come
and go, retreating when in danger. God is like
that, the girl said. We can go in and out.

Junk Pile

God throws us out the back door
onto a huge junk pile in another
galaxy. There are billions of bodies.
It's 1,000 degrees below
zero but compacted souls don't need heat.
It's logical because we
came in the front door. All of us die
in the caboose not of our choosing
but then we've always seen life
disappearing behind us, most always
into what we clumsily call the past.
Most of the girls I loved are now crones
with me a geezer, shuffling toward the moon.
So many years ago the girl with brown legs
in the green dress got off the yellow school bus.
Sometimes the past flips over and determines
what we are today. The girl's sandy
feet were on the dashboard. Beneath, thighs
were speaking the language of thighs.
Godspeed is the speed of light.

Carpe Diem

Night and day
seize the day, also the night —
a handful of water to grasp.
The moon shines off the mountain
snow where grizzlies look for a place
for the winter's sleep and birth.
I just ate the year's last tomato
in the year's fatal whirl.
This is mid-October, apple time.
I picked them for years.
One McIntosh yielded sixty bushels.
It was the birth of love that year.
Sometimes we live without noticing it.
Overtrying makes it harder.
I fell down through the tree grabbing
branches to slow the fall, got the afternoon off.
We drove her aqua Ford convertible into the country
with a sack of red apples. It was a perfect
day with her sun-brown legs and we threw ourselves
into the future together seizing the day.
Fifty years later we hold each other looking
out the windows at birds, making dinner,
a life to live day after day, a life of
dogs and children and the far wide country
out by rivers, rumpled by mountains.
So far the days keep coming.
Seize the day gently as if you loved her.

Marriage

I just remembered a serious argument.
On my seventy-fifth birthday I had the firm sense
that I was a hundred seventy-five. She disagreed.
"Look at your driver's license," she said. I said you know
the state of Montana took my license from me. She
went to my briefcase and got out my passport.
"You're a mere seventy-five," she said.
I said, "How can you trust the government
in this important matter?" I went to bed
after a couple of drinks believing I was a hundred
seventy-five. In the morning I felt
only seventy-five and apologized at breakfast.
I'd lost a hundred years and felt light,
younger, more energetic. As a boy I saw in *Life*
magazine photos of the Civil War veterans. I don't
think there are any left, are there?
They would have to be a hundred seventy-five.
Sometimes I remember aspects of that damnable war.

Round

My head is round, not perfectly so as that would be against nature. At any given time I don't know what's in it unless I pick up pen and paper and even this can be evasive. Sometimes our minds don't want to know what's in them. The girl or boy you were looking at in the coffee shop was distinctly illegal. Rebuff thoughts or go to prison, chums. Prisons no longer allow Tabasco, which could be used as a weapon or so they say. From a distance the head is a bowling ball on the shoulders, but not so: a carapace and inside, the contents are what children call "gushy." The soft brain has its own improbable life containing galaxies, tens of thousands of people met, the microcosm of life in one place and on the diaphanous and often filthy cloth of memory, hanging there and battered on the clothesline in so many years of bad weather, wet and stiff with ice or blasted by sun and heat, part of it in shreds. The bad is frankly more memorable than the good. The big truck knocking off my side-view mirror, a close call indeed. I saw his alarmed eyes, on my side of the road. I shuddered at death's door. The bowling ball is neutral but weighs the same as the head. Dropped from 35,000 feet they both can cause small earthquakes.

Dead Man's Float

Dr. Guevara said that I'm hollow-eyed
and exhausted from writing too much.
I should take a break but I don't know how.
Suddenly I remembered learning
the "dead man's float" in Boy Scout
swimming lessons and a light went off.
That's what I'll do to rest up,
the dead man's float without water.

I got in bed and conjured the feeling
of floating and recalled my last
dead man's float about a mile
out in the ocean east of Key West
when I tired from too much swimming ambition.
Big waves kept drowning my nose.
I gave up floating and swam desperately to shore.
I dozed in the hot sand and a pretty girl
stopped and asked, "Are you okay?"
"I'll never be okay," I said, and she left.
I saw her later but she wouldn't talk
to this goofy. A poet blows a chance with
a dumb witticism.

If you need me now
I'm here along the Mexican border
dead-man floating.

Barebacked Writer

When I say I'm a barebacked writer
people will start talking about horses.
I say I did that too on broad-backed June.
Her flesh hid her painful backbone so that
we could lope in the pasture in comfort.
I mean I write half-naked, shirt off,
after two years of shingles, "post-herpetic neuralgia"
where the pain is always present but can be
unbearable in a shirt, even soft cotton.
So I keep the heat high enough to go bareback
through my prose and poetry when it's snowing
outside. What is the effect except the poetry
and prose are also barebacked? Shorn of
ornament with adjectives cast in a snowbank.
Someday again I'll wear a shirt when I write
if the gods will it. For now I'm barebacked
trotting through the universe like everyone else.

Feeder

All the men grouped along the bar
like birds at the feeder at home.
The seeds of alcohol provide
a little hope and a smile or two.
These are hard times so they're sipping beer
rather than the more expensive drinks.
Sometimes I buy a round of the top stuff and
they're happy like the birds when the feeder is replenished.
Do these men live as well as birds?
It's not for me to say. They're certainly not as pretty.
They are as ordinary as house finches.
This is a story that doesn't end very well.

The Girls of Winter

Out the window of the bar I'm watching
a circle of girls stretching and yawning
across the street. It's late January and 74
degrees. They love the heat because
they *are* a moist heat. Heat loves
heat and today's a tease for what comes
with spring around here when the glorious birds
funnel back up from Mexico. The girls
don't care about birds because they *are* birds.
I recall in high school a half-dozen
cheerleaders resting on a wrestling mat
in short shorts in the gym, me beside them
with a silly groin ache. What were they?
Living, lovely, warm meat as we all are
reaching out of our bodies for someone else.

Weeks

The weeks rush past headed
for the infinity of the past, twelve billion years
ago before they had the job of being weeks.
They're tired of it and want to go back home
to a pillowed galaxy, the homeland
in the spheres with no people around
to bother them with multifoliate appointments.
Odin is welcome to stand there indefinitely
with ravens perched on his shoulders
and Vallejo to die on a rainy Thursday
in Paris after collecting discarded wine bottles
to buy bread. Bread alone only makes you
hungrier, he said. Thursday is a good day to die
especially if there's a cold rain on Montparnasse.
Vallejo wanted to go home to Peru but couldn't
with an empty wallet and a heavy heart,
seeing his soul rise over Paris up into the rain.

Time Again (2)

Time stopped at eleven a.m. Monday morning.
The fire in the mountains froze to the eye.
The Beethoven quartet on the radio continues.
Where did its sound go to become lost?
My skin tingled then stopped as it must.
Fair Catherine in the distance walks in the wheat
field, the tassels almost to her chest.
She stops and so do the sandhill cranes well ahead.
Both were adrift in this huge world,
they drifted as clouds, graceful animals,
something telling us where we're going
like migrating birds, flying into the future.

Time

Time sinks slowly to the deepest part
of the ocean, the Mariana Trench.
She's tired of light and there it's pure black.
She's also fatigued with the carcasses
of civilizations, the fleas of little lives.
She cares for children to whom she gives
more of herself willingly – their dance steps
do not drag. The very old are also
indulged with a few more days. She feels
abused by clocks. They were never meant
to be. She preferred us drifting through
our lives like clouds, without dials,
machinery, alarms, riding her
like the gentlest of horses.
Now she wants the ocean's bottom
to greet the unimaginable creatures who ignore her.

Tethered

Blacky, half Catahoula wild hog dog
and half blue heeler cow dog
has been tethered for years.
What kind of life is this?
When loose he runs into the surrounding mountains
for days on end eating what he kills.
What a choice: tethered or run away.
His girlfriend Lola, tethered across the yard,
died last week and he seems mystified.
There are rare times when
he's asked to help herd cattle in the mountains.
He becomes angry and bites the tails of calves.
His mother Lisa tore off the horn of a big bull. Tough girl.
The bull wouldn't go in the corral but swung and flung
her. They were head-to-head but she won
and carried her horn trophy around for days.
So the choice is to run into the mountains
or hang around for dinner like ordinary humans.
Some poets would run for it while most locked themselves
in universities and stayed home for dinner.
Lisa got exiled to a big ranch in Mexico.
The rancher said, "She's too much dog."

Riding the Wolf's Nose

I have the mask of a wolf's head
from Mexico. On his nose is perched
a naked, virginal girl who looks unhappy.
I imagine them running through the night
with her balanced there. The wolf
isn't reflective and doesn't know what the girl
is doing there. She had been bathing
in a pond in the forest when he picked
her up. He had to keep running or she
would get away. He doesn't know whether
to eat her or take her home to her parents.
He's heard the whole town calling for her
in the forest night and day. At dawn he dumps
her off his nose in the town's shallow fountain.
She screams at the cold water.
No one will ever believe her.

Whimsy

All I wanted when I returned from the war in China was a red-haired woman to fix me a hamburger. It was just me against twenty-five million troops. I walk through many doors that aren't there. You can't stop the molten lava coming down the mountain. Why try? Life presents us with so many impossibilities. The country boy in Kansas is in love with an actress he'll never see in *real life.* The severely crippled girl I met has never been kissed yet writes love poems. I am the bar-tailed godwit of poets. I fly 7,000 miles from the Aleutians to New Zealand without stopping. Unknown to the ornithologists I pause in China for a bowl of noodles. I can't help it. I'm full of noodle love. The same old woman puts out the bowl on her porch each year. She told me that she was once beautiful and perhaps I am a dream lover from the past. I lie back in her arms. We kiss.

The Green Man

Since early childhood I believed
in a door in the forest. I looked for it
for more than a half a century
and it evaded me. The Green Man
lived there, part tree and part human.
Keeping his distance he told me a lot.
Walk mostly sideways in the wilderness
to confuse those who would track you.
When outside, sleep with your eyes open
and see the coyote pup approach out
of curiosity, the small bear resting
against a stump a hundred yards away,
a warbler standing on your toe singing.
When I was lost he howled at me from a tree, "Wrong way."
I dreamed where he lived, high on the steep
bank of the river concealed under a thick drapery
of tree roots but I skidded on my tummy
down into the river, a sign to give up.
There was a stinking wolf den close by so my dog
wouldn't stay with me. The Green Man alone, forever.

Incidentals

Many bugs bite us.
Some snakes bite.
Birds bite bugs and seeds.
Men bite off ears in fistfights.
At dawn peeking out a cracked
window: the profusion of yellow roses
flowed over the beige stucco wall
like water. Roses bite with thorns.

Pain (2)

Pain is at the steering wheel
swerving left and right for a year now.
It costs a fortune, which I don't have,
to try to get rid of pain. Maybe a girl
could help or more vodka but I doubt it.
Or a trip to the tropics where the pain would boil away
like the hot cabin last summer where you awoke
and thought you were a corned beef boiling in a pot.
You want to give up, throw in the towel but you
can't give up because you're all you have.
Maybe they should put you down like an old dog
like our beloved cocker spaniel Mary who is nearing
the end with paralysis. Unlike me
she's happy much of the time. On walks
she keeps falling down and I pick her up
to get her started again. She seems to smile.
Neither of us wants to die
when there's work to be done,
other creatures to be snuck up on,
food to be eaten, a creek to wade,
though I hope to eventually ask God to fully
explain the meaning of Verdun where 300,000 died.

Man Dog

I envied the dog lying in the yard
so I did it. But there was a pebble
under my flank so I got up and looked
for the pebble, brushed it away
and lay back down. My dog thus far
overlooked the pebble. I guess it's her thick
Lab fur. With my head downhill the blood gorged
me with ideas. Not good. Got up. Turned around. Now I
see hundreds of infinitesimal ants. I'm on an
ant home. I get up and move five feet.
The dog hasn't moved from her serene place.
Now I'm rather too near a thicket where
I saw a big black snake last week that might decide
to join me. I moved near the actual dog this time
but she got up and went under the porch. She doesn't like
it when I'm acting weird. I'm failing as a dog
when my own kind rejects me, but doing better
than when I envied birds, the creature the least
like us, therefore utterly enviable. To be sure
I cheeped a lot but didn't try to fly.
We humans can take off but are no good at landing.

The Dog and Tobacco Room

I am the old man alone in a hotel
waiting for a ride north to Mayo Pain Clinic.
Loneliness is only a theory when we have
the past, which is a vast tumble of events.
Sort and re-sort and never win.
We live with our memories, a backpack
of mostly trash we can barely carry.
A motel in Utah gives me
the "dog and tobacco" room.
Zilpha and my cigarettes are proud.
On television I see hundreds
of cage-free piglets romping.
Things are getting better for some of us.

Notes on the Sacred Art of Log Sitting

To give the surgeon a better view of my interior carcass I was slashed from neck to tailbone. Recovery was slow and the chief neurologist told me, "You can walk your way out of this." I began walking out by shuffling down a long hallway. It was very hard on my tender empathy to see so many hopeless cases, especially the truly beautiful girl who was paralyzed for life.

I want to walk in the morning with Zilpha again. I want to walk in the morning with Zilpha again. I want to walk in the morning with Zilpha again. I want to walk in the morning with Zilpha again. I want to walk in the morning with Zilpha again. Amen.

And I want to bird hunt, which I've done with intensity for forty years in a row. Is this even possible? The answer, come to find out, was that I couldn't keep up. Zilpha would flush some birds then look to me wondering why I hadn't shot. I was far behind, sitting on an Emory oak log and staring hard at the landscape.

My shuffling mood was always corrected by sitting on an oak log, so I decided to make some notes on the sacred art of log sitting:

> Approach the log cautiously with proper reverence as if you were entering a French cathedral or the bedroom of your lover.

> If it's over 60 degrees, inspect the lower sides of the log for Mohave rattlesnakes.

> Now examine the log closely for the most comfortable place to sit, usually away from the sun.

> Sit down.

> Empty your mind of everything except what is in front of you – the natural landscape of the canyon.

Dismiss or allow to slide away any aspect of your grand or pathetic life.

Breathe softly.

Avoid a doze.

Internalize what you see in the canyon: the oaks and mesquites, the rumpled and grassy earth, hawks flying by, a few songbirds.

Stay put for forty-five minutes to an hour.

When you get up bow nine times to the log.

Three logs a day is generally my maximum.

When you get in your car it will seem as wretched as it is. A horse would be far better. For hours your mind will still be absorbed in the glory of what you saw rather than mail, e-mails, cell phones, TV, etc. Hopefully log sitting will allow you to change the contents of your life. You will introduce yourself as a "log sitter" rather than a novelist, detective, or mortician. You will walk more slowly and perhaps your feet will shuffle like mine. I can readily imagine buying a small ranch I'd call "The Log Ranch." I'd truck in thirty-three logs and arrange them on the property like the Stations of the Cross. This could soothe me during my limited time in the twenty-first century, which has been very coarse indeed. Especially after Zilpha died.

The Future (2)

Lorca was raised on his father's large
farm as a gentleman. He didn't work in the fields.
He dressed nicely and sat near ponds,
creeks, a river. In his youth he couldn't
figure out whether he liked boys or girls but boys won.
He loved birds and inevitably dreamed
of the gunshots that would kill him on the mountain,
men he knew pulling the trigger over and over.

Many of us can see our ends coming
as in a dream. Under a tree in a meadow,
or more likely, a car in the night,
balling in the bathtub when drunk,
sitting in a chair at the window
and the world slowly disappears
to music you've never heard before.
The twenty-three maenads in your life pass slowly,
some real, some imagined, of great beauty.
We never got close but they kept me alive.
They live on the mantel in my mind,
austere women shining above the fire.

Lorca Again

When Lorca was murdered
they had him turn around and look down
the steep mountainside at Granada far below.
Goodbye hometown. They shot him in the back as always,
also in the butt because he was gay. The powerful
rifles splintered him and later the family
picked up the pieces on the slope for burial.
What a rare bird. It was like shooting
the last blue heron on earth. There's a sundial
there now. We drank a bottle Christine made
called *Memoire.* I choked on the wine
and tears. At some ages he was my favorite
poet who would make me moonstruck.
I walked along the Guadalquivir in Seville
and saw his perpetual shadow in the moving
water, the local *gitano* music constricting
and exploding the heart. Water kept carrying
this burden of musical shadow to the ocean.
In the Mediterranean I heard his voice on the water.

Winter Creek

Creeks find their destiny according to the slant,
the tilt of the earth. None ever can turn around and go the other
way, at least none that I've heard of. The weight of water
and gravity are the tools. Dams are the fatal enemy
of water. You'd think the mighty Mississippi
with its trillions of tons of water would simply plummet
forward off the earth in its downhill race from Minnesota
to New Orleans. It might still happen or maybe
the Nile will fall backward and make an immense garden
of the Sahara. I sit around waiting for these things
to happen, real big thrilling things, not the greasy
soil of rotten politics but mighty bodies of water
going amok. Rain doesn't fall up but down,
the great rapids show water trying to rid
itself of earth and go back to the sky. I still
swim in rivers at night to frighten myself.
I just walked my dog to the creek where on a cold
morning she flounders and rolls happily in the mighty
mystery of moving water.

February

Warm enough here in Patagonia AZ to read
the new Mandelstam outside in my underpants
which is to say he was never warm enough
except in summer and he was without paper to write
and his belly was mostly empty most of the time
like that Mexican girl I picked up on a mountain road
the other day who couldn't stop weeping. She had slept
out two nights in a sweater in below-freezing weather.
She had been headed to Los Angeles but the *coyote*
took her money and abandoned her in the wilderness.
Her shoes were in pieces and her feet bleeding.
I took her to town and bought her food. She got a ride
to Nogales. She told us in Spanish that she just wanted
to go home and sleep in her own bed. That's what Mandelstam
wanted with mother in the kitchen fixing dinner. Everyone
wants this. Mandelstam said, "To be alone is to be alive."
"Lost and looked in the sky's asylum eye." "What of
her nights?" Maybe she was watched by some of the fifty
or so birds I have in the yard now. When they want to
they just fly away. I gave them my yard and lots of food.
They smile strange bird smiles. She couldn't fly away.
Neither can I though I've tried a lot lately to migrate
to the Camargue on my own wings. When they are married,
Mandelstam and the Mexican girl, in heaven they'll tell
long stories of the horrors of life on earth ending each session
by chanting his beautiful poems that we did not deserve.

December Butterflies

Close after dawn walking the dog,
the first yellow shafts of light shone
in the woods, and on the trail. Stand
in them and you warm up ever so little,
temperature at freezing. Saw frost on the car
windows in the driveway. Now I see
three yellow butterflies fluttering this way
so as to catch sun through the trees and
still-green willow bushes. The first hard frost kicked
the cottonwoods and now I see some of
their yellow leaves floating down the creek,
flouncing in the current. Back in Montana
it's zero and 80 mph winds.
That's why I'm here on the Mexican border.
One night here below freezing, the next day 70
degrees. This morning I feel afloat
on the creek with these leaves. Down here
the birds seem happy in winter. So am I
compared to the howling-snow-blasted north
though it's not easy to be a leaf floating in a creek.

Pool of Light

On our small front patio in this jagged landscape
there's a pool of warm light every
morning while it's still cold in the shadows
beneath a rock cliff twenty feet away.
I sit in the light for a few minutes after walking
the dog to the creek where her mind doesn't
say "creek" but mine does. I can't help it.
It occurs to me that this beloved pool of warm sun
won't last forever. It's the nature
of our nature to bid goodbye to warmth and light.
Like everything else it works for the time being,
the same as the dormant rose staring back at me.
Mind you, I'm in no rush for this to end.
I learned that after death I'll be a Chinese poet
on a ten-square-foot island and don't want to go there.
I salvaged a barrel and a piece of canvas
from the shipwreck. With lots of rain
I have sixty gallons of warm water. Migrant crabs
covered me one night and I tried to cook
them on hot rocks. Not good. I have a hook and line
but no fire so I'm eating my own brand of sushi.
If you don't love it find another universe.

Poetry Now

Poetry stinks with ten thousand poets
pissing in the same overflowing bowl.
We must go it alone, swimming at night
down the River of No Return.
At dawn we'll see unknown animals
on the bank, and unknown women, some
without faces. We're now sure that we
have both leprosy and gangrene, outcasts. After
a few nights the sight begins to fail but by now
we've earned an inner light that blossoms
in our heads. We'll talk to old Rumi
and become one with the Great Tao. We get
out on a bank and walk blindly into a forest
with our sight slowly returning. We are
now in western China and read the local old
poems. We're back in the Tang dynasty
and it takes a couple of centuries to walk
slowly to Europe reading all the way. We
stop in France and read another century
in all these great poems of Europe. When we
get home to the Midwest nobody recognizes
us but we have learned the cosmos of poetry.

Criticism

Like a bird dog my blood is a dictator.
I've had no choice in this matter. They put
me down in a grand field and I was off and running
for the unruly birds, poems, looking in a dozen nearly
impenetrable thickets. I'm also a hangman
for my bad poems. String them up, dammit,
from the old clothesline where the wind
will whip them to shreds. Our local wind
tips over trucks with its fury. It can easily
shred bad poems to tiny chicken feathers.

Money

The 8,000 isn't coming now and won't ever.
I had counted on those birds in the bush.
This mud bath doesn't smear the landscape,
but it is a huge pothole in my road –
it can break an axle or cause a blowout –
deep with sharp edges.
On my hands and knees I stared
into this pothole thinking
of the black holes in outer space –
then one was on the ground right in front of me.
The money hole I called it, like
the willow shadows of late October,
dark and cold and then a few feet away
you can walk into morning sunlight
where the frost is melting, and up to
my bench in the pasture
where money doesn't exist.
The mountains on the moon
were so bright last night.

Money on the moon? I don't think so.
Money is listless and lives in total dark.
Money can be slightly soiled and disrupting.
Money can buy valuable things such as macaroni and wine.
Money is the major pothole of my life.

Bird Nightmares

The worst dream ever that all the birds in the world died overnight. Science couldn't figure it out but then a humble graduate student from Caltech said that a prodigious number of quasar particles were speeding toward earth at 5,000 miles per second. These particles supposedly pass through us harmlessly from a galaxy that had a black hole the equal in power to five billion suns. Is God thinking too big? I wondered. So the birds were destroyed by this surge in cosmic power. Bird-watching groups committed suicide en masse. They were in a medieval hell without birds. It was soon discovered that the quasars were reducing human intelligence by a fatal half. Minor wars broke out everywhere in the world. Luckily no one was bright enough to press the red button. Dogs ate dogs. Married couples murdered each other in great numbers to no surprise. Animals went berserk, unlike us they couldn't adjust to being stupid. People were reduced to reading poetry because it was shorter. A raven on the verge of death said to me, "Why did you do this to us?" The same question they always ask us. A few swallows were found in Brazil deep in a cove behind a giant waterfall. Brazil kept these for themselves, wanting to be the only country with birds. There was money in it. Thousands died trying to visit the birds. The waterfall made Niagara look like a trickle. Many stayed with the birds until they starved to death.

He Dog

I'm a very old dog,
much older than most dogs.
I can't give out my wisdom
because I bark loudly and virtually
no one understands this barking except
a few other dogs of my peculiar species.
I don't bark at cars. They're beneath contempt.
I bark at the rising sun when it rises
red out of a forest fire.
I bark at thunder out of pure envy,
the mighty noise this sky dog makes.
I growl at myself when I sleep too much
and don't run to the far field in the morning
where I saw the bear bigger than me and ran home.
I don't bark at the night. I love its black music.
I sleep under the porch, inside during winter.
Once I had a girlfriend for the day.
I have puppies but I don't know where.

Tree Coroner

When we have rare big winds down here
trees blow over, almost always the cottonwoods
which are huge but short-rooted, while mesquite
taproots go down seventy-five feet, and
the Emory oaks are also solid. I wander around
examining the fallen trees for causes.
Most often like people there is rot
inside. The other day one was rotted six feet
through the trunk, which was utterly ripped
and twisted with the roots above ground, the torsion
force incredible and you wouldn't want
to be there to get driven like a nail into the ground.
Tree coroner isn't an elected office
where my dark past would confuse voters like Joyce Kilmer,
who thought a poem couldn't be as lovely as a tree.
Grow up, Joyce, you're comparing apples to oranges.
This is one of those things you've got to know.

Books

Looking around this casita and the house
in Montana I see I must have bought
thousands of books. Of course many came
free from people to irritate me with guilt
for not reading so many galleys and manuscripts.
It's plain as day that I've vastly overfed
my brain. At this age it's a dense jungle
and I can't write ten points of wisdom
for you to grease your skids on the way
to our mutual doom. A few years ago
my living motto was "Eat or Die" but now
that's worn out, too tired to guide my clumsy
way from pillar to post to pit of despond.
I must sell these books, some quite rare,
or exchange them for good food and the wine
I can no longer afford. I used to look
at pages 33, 77, 153 for the secrets of the world
and never find them but still continue trying.

Patagonia AZ

A little rain at dawn after months
of drought. The dust holds
the smell of rain tight to its chest.
In the rocks I hear the voice
of a girl from fifty years ago.
Down here you listen to mountains.

Melrose (2)

A long freight train is parked out front.
A thunderstorm comes across the mountains,
not a huge one just a regular thunderstorm.
I'd like to have rain on this tin roof,
an early memory that soothed my blind eye,
hot and raw in my head at our little cabin
on a lake. That and catching so many fish
for the family to eat. I was only seven and proud
to catch dinner. Many pans full of bluegills
and perch all brown and tasty. "Watch out, the bones
can kill you," I'd say, having heard it from adults
over and over. The splendor of hard rain falling,
which is now. Me and my young-boy hard-on
wondering what I'd do on earth because that's all
I had. Maybe be a hero, or if that's difficult, a farmer.

Dark

By miracle night arrived
along with the liquid dark.
I like it best while camping
at first you see the dimming lake
and then you can't see ten feet
past the fire. At dawn you're reassured
by the first trickle of light
from the east. I love its paleness
though the day becomes blazing
the tent too hot for a nap. I sit in the shade
of a cliff, watch a big rattler come
out of its hole, wait a few minutes,
go back in the hole, too hot for a rattler.
I drink all my water on the three-mile
way back to the car, drive a couple of hours
to Tucson from this wretched desert, an outdoorsman
with a credit card. I check in at the Ramada
and sleep all day in the air-conditioning,
the TV said it was 107 today. All night
I heard yodeling angels, likely a pack of coyotes
crisscrossing the dark. I carry a gun
because I'm a fearful human. A thousand
times I awoke to think of a beautiful girl
who died in Flint, Michigan. A disease quickly ate
her up. If she had been with me I couldn't have
stopped death. We would have sung songs of mourning
all night long. Also laughter in the dark. At dawn
as a dog breathes, so breathe I.

Sunday

On a Sunday morning walk I carry a pistol
having seen a big rattler on the path yesterday.
I don't want to lose my beloved dog, Zil.
I lost my setter Rose to them, a fang in the eye
and one in the cheek. She suffered horribly.
I therefore declared jihad against them
when they're close to the house
in favor of grandchildren and dogs.
They are so startling as if our blood
understands the rattle. I have teased
them with my walking stick and am amazed
how far they can strike with their fat, curled bodies.
At heart I don't want to kill on the Lord's day.

Cattle Nap

How lovely the sleeping Black Angus cows
in the green, green pasture. They start
eating at dawn in the first pale light,
then when the heat gathers midmorning
they all flop down, sprawling in naps
except a few calves who don't want
a nap and wander around bothering everyone
but they are ignored and finally sleep.
The bull calves wake up first, spar and butt heads
in imitation of future sexual wars,
"I'm biggest and strongest I want all the females,"
but now all becomes peaceful on a somnolent
summer day, lumps of black in the green
pasture, a hundred or so, large and small
and then as if on signal they get up and start eating.
Why does this so please me? Like ourselves
it's important that these doomed creatures are
ignorant of the future and remain peacefully
with nature eating the thick green grass.

Life

I'm not so good at life anymore.
Sometimes I wake up and don't recognize it.
Houses, cars, furniture, books are a blur
while trees, birds, and horses are fine
and clear. I also understand music
of an ancient variety – pre-ninteenth century.
Where have I been?
Recounting flowers from the train window
between Seville and Granada, also bulls and olive trees.
I couldn't sleep in Lorca's room because it was haunted.
Even the wine I carried was haunted.
Spain has never recovered from this murder.
Her nights are full of the red teeth of death.
There were many who joined him. You can't count,
up and down, birds and flowers at the same time.

Universe

The landscape above confuses me.
Only twice have I seen Venus drowning
in the cup of the new moon.
I want to read it like a sky-
high book and know what's beyond.
Seeing is believing.
I'm told there's no last page.
It's just black and lasts forever. At church
they said that each year is a single grain
of sand and when the beaches of the world
are used up eternity is just getting started
so you don't want to spend that time in hell.
Machado said that the indifferent water holds
the stars in its heart. Precisely. I can only
study the universe on the surface
of a calm lake way back in the forest,
where the speed of light comes to a dead stop.
Buried in water the stars move very slowly.

Herring

I'm sitting at the window eating pickled herring
and watching the existence of earth.
A small brown bird flies in from the left,
a fellow creature. We are each other
though he's more closely related
to dinosaurs. Lucky for us
this existence doesn't include
the future, which at this point is questionable.
Israel and Iran bomb each other at the same
split second. Thousands
of small brown birds will die in what
the media call *conflagration,* temporarily the world's
biggest double bonfire. I won't attend the party.
It's far too small for God to see
in a universe with ninety billion galaxies
small brown birds and herring.

Things Unseen

When I was a child they'd sing at church, "I love to tell the story of unseen things above." The Lord sat on a throne of pearl, gold, diamonds but my dad said take this with a grain of salt. The Lord spent forty days in the wilderness, that's what he liked. After church out in the yard I'd stare straight up in hopes of seeing these unseen things above. You couldn't stand out in the parking lot because big Christians were swerving out headed for the Pancake House. This was an after-church ritual. A huge plate of pancakes drowning in syrup to compensate for a boring sermon. I knew the son of the owners of the Pancake House who said that these sugar-freak Christians go through expensive gallons of syrup on Sunday mornings. My family never went because of the expense. When we got home we'd change clothes and my father would stand at the stove to make his favorite buckwheat pancakes and a pan of sausage. We'd have homemade maple syrup made from thirty maples in the yard. This was good enough for us. He said those people knock themselves out and can't work in the garden until late afternoon. Drink a quart of syrup and see what happens to you. I still stare at the sky for signs of heavens but without the help of syrup.

Cigarette

With earth you wonder whether God lit
the wrong end of the cigarette, tossed it aside.
But no, we were magnificent once.
Now we humans are vile machines of attrition.
Nothing escapes our notice, even the butterflies
in the Amazon that must get their salt
from the tears of turtles are a possible profit
for window displays, salt ads,
a fortune in butterflies drinking tears.

Nuthatch Girl

The gods lost footing and rolled down
the mountain into a heap at the bottom.

We have to do thus and so to keep
them alive.

Everyone forgot their assignment
except a young girl from Missouri
who danced down a cliff bare naked.

She's part bird so it was cheating a little.

Gods encourage supernatural cheating.

Meanwhile the girl climbed up a tree
like a nuthatch to read Rumi aloud
in his original language.

It's up to poets to revive the gods.

Big Issues

All these planted flowers
I stare at every day have become
part of my brain. Outside the studio door
twelve poppies, seven peonies.
The numbers change nearly every day.
Are they doing damage
keeping me from all the big issues?
Of course, but the big issues don't need me.
The surrounding mountains are a real big
issue. To them my steps are soft as a moth's.
There are too many people for me to be a big
issue. I'm more on the level of a crow.
The sixteen poppies and eight peonies are getting in the way
of the United Nations, existentialism, and masculinity.
These big issues all fade in the face of beauty.

Apple

I just picked and ate the first apple
of the year, slightly sour, from a low-hanging
branch. There was a deep peck hole
from a magpie I ate around. Me and the birds,
deer, the apple herself, are lucky to have apples in our world.
The biggest branch broke off in a storm and we lost
a third of the harvest, like the dog eating rabbits
and duck eggs. Nature gets bruised, injured,
murdered in bed. But now staring into the greenery
there are hundreds of apples slowly turning rose.
We are saved from apple hunger.

Sundial

Startled by the earth at dawn.
It was far too green.
The horse was a wet gray.
The birds were too loud.
I touched a veronica flower
with my eyelash.
The snake tested the air
with its tongue.
The mountain across the river
is in flames, a week now.
This isn't a dream.
I heard the sounds of all doors
of earth opening and closing.
You can't close a door on the river.
We drank wine on the mountainside
next to Lorca's memorial sundial.
A house was burning in Granada.
The train went north toward Seville
where the Guadalquivir waited for it to cross.
Someone dropped an olive in the grass.
A boy played a guitar on a rooftop,
which made me weep tears
the exact temperature of life.

Winter, Spring

Winter is black and beige down here
from drought. Suddenly in March
there's a good rain and in a couple
of weeks we are enveloped in green.
Green everywhere in the mesquites, oaks,
cottonwoods, the bowers of thick
willow bushes the warblers love
for reasons of food or the branches,
the tiny aphids they eat with relish.

Each year it is a surprise
that the world can turn green again.
It is the grandest surprise in life,
the birds coming back from the south to my open
arms, which they fly past, aiming at the feeders.

April

Still April though the last day.
So many days are somber here with darkish
clouds floating through the mountains. At night
cold rain falls turning to snow in the mountains,
which crawls down to the valley bringing a taste
of winter again. People say "Oh no" having had
a rough winter. The grizzly bears have emerged
from their dens wondering, "What's there to eat,"
which they haven't done in five months.
Down here it's green under the slight
blanket of snow. I brush it off my peonies.

Tiny Bird

The urge to be a tiny bird
upon a tiny limb, maybe
a bridled titmouse
standing on its spidery feet,
not a big guy who falls
with a resounding thump
and bruises sidewalks and pastures,
sinks in river mud to the waist.
If my feet were spears I would have descended
to one of the tumultuous underground rivers which are
everywhere, earthborn by the black current.
When young I thought I'd die in my thirties
like so many of my favorite poets.
At seventy-five I see this hasn't happened.
Still, I am faithful to my poems and birds.
Birds are poems I haven't caught yet.

Apple Tree

Sitting under the apple tree on a hot
June day harassed by blackbirds
and a house wren who have nests there.
I'm thinking of the future and the past,
and how the past at my age has become
obviously so much longer than the future.
This feeling always precedes my sense
that severe weather is coming. I don't believe
in doom or destiny – I believe in turmoil,
thunderstorms in the head, rolling lightning
coming down my brain's road. As an artist
you follow the girl in the white tennis dress
for 25,000 miles and never close the deal.

Galactic

Sitting out in my chair near Linda's garden.
A mixture of flowers and vegetables, pink iris,
wild poppies, roses, blue salvia and veronica
among tomatoes, green beans, eggplant and onion.
I think that I sense the far-flung galaxies
and hear a tinge of the solar winds.
Where is my dead brother? I want to know.
With so many infirmities I await the miraculous.
Galaxies are grand thickets of stars
in which we may hide forever.

The River

Yes, we'll gather by the river,
the beautiful, the beautiful river.
They say it runs by the throne of God.
This is where God invented fish.
Wherever, but then God's throne is as wide
as the universe. If you're attentive you'll
see the throne's borders in the stars. We're on this side
and when you get to the other side we don't know
what will happen if anything. If nothing happens
we won't know it, I said once. Is that cynical?
No, nothing is nothing, not upsetting just
nothing. Then again maybe we'll be cast
at the speed of light through the universe
to God's throne. His hair is bounteous.
All the 5,000 birds on earth were created there.
The firstborn cranes, herons, hawks, at the back
so as not to frighten the little ones.
Even now they remember this divine habitat.
Shall we gather at the river, this beautiful river?
We'll sing with the warblers perched on his eyelashes.

Daylight

Did you notice the daylight today?
These days are short in December.
It comes before dark. Sometimes it passes
in a hurry to get someplace else
more friendly, perhaps. Fiji, maybe.
We become forgetful and miss it some days.
In March there were six different warblers
in one willow bush. What else could
you possibly want from daylight?

Warbler

This year we have two gorgeous
yellow warblers nesting in the honeysuckle bush.
The other day I stuck my head in the bush.
The nestlings weigh one-twentieth of an ounce,
about the size of a honeybee. We stared at
each other, startled by our existence.
In a month or so, when they reach the size
of bumblebees they'll fly to Costa Rica without a map.

The Final List

They want to operate on me again.
They took away my driver's license.
I can go nowhere to get food and wine.
Thousands of buds fell to the grass
from the apple and crabapple trees.
The apple buds are white against green grass.
The crabapple buds are bright pink.
They see it coming. It happens every year.
They are happily enough flowers for the void.

A Dog in Heaven

An ancient problem never solved until this moment.
Did Jesus have a dog with him
during the forty days in the wilderness?
Yes. In the village the dog was called Cain
in jest. He would eat anything he could get
in his mouth. He would try to make love to chickens
to the laughter of the children who threw stones
at him, a great sin to throw stones at poor
stray dogs. So when Jesus left the village
at dawn with a loaf of bread and a bedroll
Cain followed and Jesus didn't have the heart
to yell "Go away" to the woe-begotten Cain.
So Cain trailed happily along and at the end
of the first hot day he stopped, sniffed the air.
He turned left and waited for Jesus to follow.
Cain led the way down a gorge to a spring he knew.
The spring emerged from a tiny cave in the cliff.
Cain and Jesus drank deeply and he filled his container.
Then they bathed in the cool water. At twilight they
were next to the north shore of the Sea of Galilee.
Jesus caught a fine fish with a hook and line he had packed
cooking it on a flat rock where they had built a fire.
He picked a bone out of the dog's gum. A few years later
he told Cain to stay home because he had to be crucified
in Jerusalem. He actually put Cain in the tomb
with a chunk of camel meat and said he'd come back to get
him. On the third day Jesus's tomb was empty.
Cain had been invited along for the Resurrection ride.

Quarantine

I've been quarantined by the gods.
Do no harm, they said.
Tell no secrets. I had stored
my spirit in the big willow tree to the west
of my study on the advice of Rumi.
It was getting badly bruised every day
and my spirit needed a resting place.
I forgot where I put it when you
should check it every morning.
I sank lower and lower until one day
I called it back from the tree
then wrote a pretty good poem.
There is no time to fool around, the gods said.
They blew my poem with the wind to
the top of Antelope Butte. I can't walk there
with my cane. Some gods have been dead
a thousand years and need our magic
and music to come back to life.
We owe it to them. They got us started.

Moon Suite

The moon came to the forge
with her skirt of white, fragrant flowers.
The young boy watches her, watches.
The boy is watching her.
FEDERICO GARCÍA LORCA

The full moon is rising from her nest
high in the Absaroka mountains –
a miraculous cliché
shining down, glistening,
on thousands of acres of hay.

~

The new moon, how I loved it
out over the still lake in childhood.
It meant a fresh start whirring
in from the sky with the nightjars,
bullbats, and ten thousand swallows
to eat the mosquitoes you were breathing.

~

Seeing the moon the loon began to call
and a few stars seemed to hiss.
When we were young on the lake the night
was alive, bobcat yowl, buck deer snort,
a thousand irritable birds, the hum of night
herself holding her weight of stars and moon.
Dawn only came when the night was exhausted.

~

Brother said the moon was a mushroom
feeding on light until it got white and fat.
Astronomers say this is true.

~

The moon was sitting on the hill
behind the house
so I walked right into it –
cold and soft and not bright white
as you might think, more cream-colored
with a warm wind.
I thought I might see John Keats.

~

The big moon rose
through the forest fire across the river.
I had a primitive fear she was aflame.
An older man was caught camping up there
and had to hike with his old dog Brownie
across the divide ahead of the chasing fire.
They made it in the burning moonlight.

~

"Walking in Jerusalem just like John"
but farther east in the desert.
In the moonlight you could see mating vipers.
They were everywhere in old Bible pictures
at the feet of the saints but didn't strike them.

~

In the Far East we worried about immense tigers
eating the moon, its pieces falling from their jaws.

~

You can't rearrange the heavens to suit
yourself. Even the gods are powerless
with sun, moon, and planets. Wildflowers
listen carefully to the gods and also to sea lions.
Perhaps the gods want us to be wildflowers.
Surprises on earth, these wildflowers.
We can't seem to change anything anywhere.

~

The stars have been getting too large lately,
big white loose splotches in a liquid sky.
Can I handle this jigsaw puzzle
of the universe? I'll need a thousand
dog teams and very long ropes.
There'll be no seating for the audience
they must stand in the nation's backyards.
Earth will be at peace again through dog power.
The International Dog Church will be founded.
The moon will be called Holy Dog Moon,
the sun called Sun Dog.
The gods are now called dogs and are much happier.
Marching is permanently banished in favor of trotting.

~

The bear broke free from his constellation
and loped through the cosmos thinking
he scented a female in a distant world.

~

Our difficult selves are cast in iron.
Only the most extreme heat makes us malleable.

~

All my life I've been a night bird.
Thousands of evenings looking at thousands
of acres of black windows. What's out there?
Everything from murderers to ghosts
and gods who are safe from us in the dark.
The gulley is full of big green willow bushes
waiting patiently for the tiny migrant warblers
due in a few weeks. The stars don't
know who we are. The slim new moon
rising strains to capture Venus in her
curve. Sometimes I'm inside and
outside at the same time. Blackness is a friend
concealing my disfigurement from private wars.

~

Last night the big moon carved me up
with her invisible white knives. In the dark
yard I chanted and flopped. Where is my
straitjacket when I need it? I held on to
a willow so as not to be taken up in the air.
I can't leave earth tonight, I pleaded.
We always say *not yet* to the gods,
who get irritable when they can't kill us.

~

A new moon with Venus nearby
though not in the moon cup as I'd prefer her.
So hard to organize these things.
Yahweh is the God of galaxies
while the moon rolls freely to help the oceans
and to haunt us with our life before birth,
in a different kingdom far away.

~

We swam at night
under the moon's reflection
and tried to catch her.
She slipped through our fingers.

~

The moon stares at me impolitely
through the fir trees and the willow and window.
She's like that. Staring back
you can trip in the yard.

~

The full moon caught herself in the contorted rose vines
beyond the window. The rose is called Madame Alfred Carrière,
bred for climbing castle walls. We only have
a little casita, a gatehouse, but the huge rose
is here just the same for peasants.
I am not strong enough to disentangle the moon.

Nobody is.

~

We were frightened last October when a big wind
from the north scudded the moon back south
where it was prayed for, needed by Día de Muertos.
What fun to dance, get drunk in a cemetery.
An immense angel died, fell draped over the mountains
imagining snow. We missed the full moon.

~

Once I heard wolves in full moonlight.
A huge storm visited the cabin, also green northern lights.
The sky split open in the west, and beyond the storm
the wolves were howling within the thunder.
The earth was forcing me to not forget her.
I never recovered from that night.
This all would never happen again.

~

The last moon will be black in the red sky.
The last girl will weigh two sparrow feathers.
At my age you don't think about the future
because you don't have one.

~

Up close
the moon
fills the world.

Bridge

Most of my life was spent
building a bridge out over the sea
though the sea was too wide.
I'm proud of the bridge
hanging in the pure sea air. Machado
came for a visit and we sat on the
end of the bridge, which was his idea.

Now that I'm old the work goes slowly.
Ever nearer death, I like it out here
high above the sea bundled
up for the arctic storms of late fall,
the resounding crash and moan of the sea,
the hundred-foot depth of the green troughs.
Sometimes the sea roars and howls like
the animal it is, a continent wide and alive.
What beauty in this the darkest music
over which you can hear the lightest music of human
behavior, the tender connection between men and galaxies.

So I sit on the edge, wagging my feet above
the abyss. Tonight the moon will be in my lap.
This is my job, to study the universe
from my bridge. I have the sky, the sea, the faint
green streak of Canadian forest on the far shore.

About the Author

Jim Harrison is one of America's most versatile and celebrated writers. He is the author of thirty-six books of poetry, fiction, and nonfiction – including *Legends of the Fall,* the acclaimed trilogy of novellas, and *The Shape of the Journey: New and Collected Poems.* A member of the American Academy of Arts and Letters, he divides his time between western Montana and southern Arizona.

Poetry is vital to language and living. Since 1972, Copper Canyon Press has published extraordinary poetry from around the world to engage the imaginations and intellects of readers, writers, booksellers, librarians, teachers, students, and donors.

WE ARE GRATEFUL FOR THE MAJOR SUPPORT PROVIDED BY:

THE PAUL G. ALLEN
FAMILY FOUNDATION

CULTURE

*Special thanks are due to the following individuals
for their generous support of this publication:*

Bruce S. Kahn

Gregg Orr

Peter Phinny

TO LEARN MORE ABOUT UNDERWRITING
COPPER CANYON PRESS TITLES,
PLEASE CALL 360-385-4925 EXT. 103

WE ARE GRATEFUL FOR THE MAJOR SUPPORT PROVIDED BY:

Anonymous

John Branch

Diana Broze

Beroz Ferrell & The Point, LLC

Janet and Les Cox

Mimi Gardner Gates

Linda Gerrard and Walter Parsons

Gull Industries, Inc.
on behalf of William and Ruth True

Mark Hamilton and Suzie Rapp

Carolyn and Robert Hedin

Steven Myron Holl

Lakeside Industries, Inc.
on behalf of Jeanne Marie Lee

Maureen Lee and Mark Busto

Brice Marden

Ellie Mathews and Carl Youngmann
as The North Press

H. Stewart Parker

Penny and Jerry Peabody

John Phillips and Anne O'Donnell

Joseph C. Roberts

Cynthia Lovelace Sears and
Frank Buxton

The Seattle Foundation

Kim and Jeff Seely

David and Catherine Eaton Skinner

Dan Waggoner

C.D. Wright and Forrest Gander

Charles and Barbara Wright

The dedicated interns and faithful volunteers of Copper Canyon Press

~

This book is set in Dante, a typeface designed
in 1954 by Giovanni Mardersteig, based on
fifteenth-century types of Francesco Griffo. Over
the years it has been reworked by Monotype for
machine and digital composition. The book title
is set in Quadraat Sans, a contemporary typeface
by Fred Smeijers. Book design and composition
by VJB/Scribe. Printed on archival-quality paper.

Dead Man's Float is also issued in a signed, limited
edition of 150 numbered copies and 26 lettered
copies. These limited editions are available exclu-
sively through donation to Copper Canyon Press.
Please e-mail gifts@coppercanyonpress.org for
more details.